Scripture Sessions on the New Testament

Pray It! Study It! Live It!® resources offer a holistic approach to learning, living, and passing on the Catholic faith.

Scripture Sessions on the New Testament

Participant Workbook

Tony Tamberino

Saint Mary's Press®

Genuine recycled paper with 10% post-consumer waste. 5099400

The publishing team included Laurie Delgatto and Brian Singer-Towns, development editors; Lorraine Kilmartin, reviewer; Mary Koehler, permissions editor; prepress and manufacturing coordinated by the prepublication and production services departments of Saint Mary's Press.

Copyright © 2006 by Saint Mary's Press, Christian Brothers Publications, 702 Terrace Heights, Winona, MN 55987-1318, www.smp.org. All rights reserved. No part of this book may be reproduced by any means without the written permission of the publisher.

Printed in the United States of America

Printing: 9 8 7 6 5 4 3 2 1

Year: 2014 13 12 11 10 09 08 07 06

ISBN-13: 978-0-88489-866-5
ISBN-10: 0-88489-866-0

Contents

Introduction 7

1
Reading the Bible as Catholics 9

2
Introduction to the Gospels 12

3
The Synoptic Gospels 18

4
The Gospel of John 22

5
Acts and Galatians: The Universality of Christianity 26

6
Romans and James: Faith 31

7
The Book of Revelation: Our Ultimate Destiny 35

8
Truth in the Bible 40

Acknowledgments 44

No part of this book may be reproduced by any means.

INTRODUCTION

STUDYING THE SCRIPTURES

WHY STUDY THE BIBLE?

Why do we *study* the Bible? If it is God's truth, can't we just read the words and immediately "get" what they mean?

The fact is that some of the Bible can be puzzling to modern ears. We may not understand the circumstances under which the texts were written or the meaning intended by the authors. Some of the material might seem contradictory. These traits are particularly true of the Old Testament, whose origins are complex.

In a literal sense, the Bible has been translated from the Hebrew and the Greek into a number of English versions. The translation we speak of here includes study that is aimed at discovering an author's original intent in writing a given scriptural text. Once we see what the author meant—and this takes some understanding of the circumstances at that time—we can appreciate what God is saying to us today through these texts.

The purpose of studying the Scriptures is not simply that we might know a lot of things about the Bible or even its theological meaning. Knowledge is important and useful but not enough. The deeper intent of Scripture study is that we "fall in love" with the Bible and with God, who is its source and inspiration.

WHY THE NEW TESTAMENT?

> But as for you, continue in what you have learned and firmly believed, knowing from whom you learned it, and how from childhood you have known the sacred writings that are able to instruct you for salvation through faith in Christ Jesus. All scripture is inspired by God and is useful for teaching, for reproof, for correction, and for training in righteousness, so that everyone who belongs to God may be proficient, equipped for every good work. (2 Timothy 3:14–17)

Timothy was a young Christian leader, and this passage from the New Testament is addressed to him. He is encouraged to use the Scriptures as a basis for his life. The author tells Timothy that the Scriptures can be used for teaching, for living morally, and for growing spiritually.

The need to build a life based on the Scriptures is just as important today as it was for people during the time Second Timothy was written. God's revelation in the

Scriptures provides answers to life's crucial questions. And just like Timothy, each of us can explore the Scriptures to find the guidance we need.

This course is designed to give you a foundation for a solid Catholic understanding of Scripture. The sessions in this workbook will challenge you to study the New Testament with purpose, to read and proclaim the word of God with faith, and to live that word in every moment.

For each session offered at your parish or school, this workbook has corresponding activities that include Scripture readings, commentaries, reflection and discussion questions, ideas to think about, and topics to discuss with your fellow faith-sharers, friends, and family members.

1
READING THE BIBLE AS CATHOLICS

Reading and studying the Bible can be a daunting task, particularly for those whose experience is limited to Sunday liturgy or religion classes. Often we are confused about how to understand the sacred Scriptures and are unaware that not all Christians approach studying and praying the Bible in the same way. During this session we will examine some factors Catholics should keep in mind as they encounter God's word.

THE SCRIPTURES

> But Timothy has just now come to us from you, and has brought us the good news of your faith and love. He has told us also that you always remember us kindly and long to see us—just as we long to see you. For this reason, brothers and sisters, during all our distress and persecution we have been encouraged about you through your faith. For we now live, if you continue to stand firm in the Lord. How can we thank God enough for you in return for all the joy that we feel before our God because of you? Night and day we pray most earnestly that we may see you face to face and restore whatever is lacking in your faith.
>
> Now may our God and Father himself and our Lord Jesus direct our way to you. And may the Lord make you increase and abound in love for one another and for all, just as we abound in love for you. And may he so strengthen your hearts in holiness that you may be blameless before our God and Father at the coming of our Lord Jesus with all his saints. (1 Thessalonians 3:6–13)

ENCOURAGEMENT

> Sometimes, we feel alone in our faith. We wonder if anyone feels, thinks, or prays the way we do. As a first missionary of the faith, Paul must have experienced his share of dark days when he wondered if the people would really accept the Good News. He must have been so encouraged when Timothy returned to tell him of the "faith and love" of the Thessalonians (1 Thessalonians 3:6).
>
> The Christian faith is never meant to be held privately. We don't grow in our faith, hope, and love by being isolated from other people. Like Paul, we need the encouragement and challenge of other people; our family, friends, and the entire Christian community. (*The Catholic Youth Bible*®, near 1 Thessalonians 3:6–13)

A Community Faithful to Tradition

Complete the following information about the person whose name you have chosen:
- the time in which she or he lived

- one or two things the person did

- the person's importance in the history of salvation

For Reflection

- Write a journal prayer to the Holy Spirit asking for the grace of inspiration and faithfulness to the Word of God.

- What, in your opinion, is the biggest advantage to being part of the Catholic community?

- Make a list of other important aspects of the Catholic approach to the Bible.

Live It!

- Interview your pastor about his role and responsibility as the leader and guardian of the parish.
- Talk to a friend from another Christian faith about his or her understanding of the Bible. How does your friend understand biblical inspiration? Is there an authority in his or her faith that guides its interpretation of Scripture for the community? How important is the community in its members' understanding of their own call to follow Jesus? When they read or study the Bible, are they aware of things like literary forms?
- Suggest that a short reading from the Bible be shared occasionally at family meals at Sunday dinner or during Advent and Lent. Perhaps each person could share a thought about the reading with the group.

2
INTRODUCTION TO THE GOSPELS

An integral part of biblical education for Catholics is an introduction to Catholic approaches for interpreting the Bible. All of us need to understand the importance of interpreting the Bible in context so we are equipped to deal with biblical fundamentalism. The Gospels are a fertile source for understanding issues such as how the Bible was written, the historical situation of the Bible authors' community, and the awareness of different literary forms in the Bible.

THE SCRIPTURES

> Since many have undertaken to set down an orderly account of the events that have been fulfilled among us, just as those who were eyewitnesses from the beginning and servants of the word have handed them down to us, I too decided, after investigating everything carefully from the very first, to write an orderly account for you, most excellent Theophilus, so that you may know the truth concerning the things about which you have been instructed. (Luke 1:1–4)

STAGES IN THE FORMATION OF THE GOSPELS

AD 27–30 Jesus's Preaching and Public Ministry
  AD 30 Jesus's Death and Resurrection

AD 30–70 Apostolic Preaching
  Early Communities Living the Gospel
  Jerusalem Council (AD 50)
  Paul's Missionary Journeys
    and Letters (AD 46–62)

AD 65–100 Writing of the Gospels
  Mark (AD 65–70)
  Luke (AD 80–85)
  Matthew (AD 85)
  John (AD 90–100)

Literary Forms in the Gospels

- genealogy

- historical background

- teaching passages

- prayers

- miracle stories

- parables

- allegories (This is like that.)

- Passion (suffering and death) stories

- Resurrection stories

PHILIPPIANS 2:5–11

All:
> You must have the attitude of Christ Jesus.

Right:
> Who, though he was in the form of God,
>> did not regard equality with God
>> as something to be exploited.

Left:
> But emptied himself,
>> taking the form of a slave,
>> being born in human likeness.

All:
> You must have the attitude of Christ Jesus.

Right:
> And found in human form,
>> he humbled himself
>> and became obedient to the point of death—
>> even death on a cross.

Left:
> Therefore God also highly exalted him
>> and gave him the name
>> that is above every name.

All:
> You must have the attitude of Christ Jesus.

Right:
> So that at the name of Jesus
>> every knee should bend,
>> in heaven and on earth and under the earth.

Left:
> And every tongue should confess
>> to the glory of God the Father:

All:
> JESUS CHRIST IS LORD!
> You must have the attitude of Christ Jesus.

(This prayer is adapted from Philippians 2:5–11.)

The Events of the Passion

- The Agony in the Garden
- The Betrayal and Arrest
- Jesus Before the High Priest
- Peter's Denial
- The Crucifixion
- The Soldiers Mock Jesus
- Jesus Before Pilate
- The Death of Jesus

Luke's Account of Jesus's Death

The stories of Jesus's Passion—the name Christians use to describe his suffering and death—differ in all four Gospels. By comparing these stories, we gain insight into the authors' portrayals of Jesus. Let's take a closer look at the perspective of the Gospel of Luke. First, in Jesus's Passion, Luke describes the openness of the Gentiles to Jesus's message of salvation. For example, Pilate finds Jesus innocent three times in Luke (23:4,14,22) and hands him over to be crucified only at the insistence of the Jewish leaders (verse 24). Later, it is a Roman centurion who praises God at the moment of Jesus's death (verse 47). Second, Luke emphasizes Jesus's compassion and forgiveness, even during his greatest suffering. While carrying the cross, Jesus shows his concern for the women who are following him (verses 28–31). As he is nailed to the cross, he forgives those responsible (verse 34). And when one of the criminals asks for Jesus to remember him, Jesus goes beyond that to promise him the first place in Paradise (verse 43). Third, Luke emphasizes Jesus's glory and divinity. Whereas Mark portrays Jesus abandoned in his Passion (Mark 15:34), Luke surrounds Jesus with sympathetic people: a crowd including the women of Jerusalem (Luke 23:27), the good thief (verses 40–41), and the centurion (verse 47). In Mark, Jesus feels God's absence (Mark 15:34), but Luke presents Jesus in control even at his death, handing his spirit over to God (Luke 23:46). Luke is making it clear in his portrayal of Jesus's Passion that Jesus is the loving, forgiving savior of all humankind. (*The Catholic Youth Bible*, near Luke 22:47—23:56)

The Jesus Prayer

Lord, Jesus Christ,
Son of the Living God,
Have Mercy on Me,
A sinner.

For Reflection

- Make a journal entry about what you would say to Jesus as he hangs on the cross.

- List the people and the reasons that help you believe in the Resurrection.

Live It!

- View the film *Absence of Malice* (1981, 116 minutes, rated PG). The movie deals with media responsibility for what and how it publishes information.
- Invite older members of your extended family for an evening of dinner and storytelling. Make it an opportunity for people to ask about the "things they always wanted to know."
- Plan a trip to the local cathedral to examine its artistic renderings of Jesus.
- Instead of a family movie night, occasionally have a short-story night. Each person reads a favorite short story and then everyone shares his or her favorite part of the story.

3
THE SYNOPTIC GOSPELS

The three synoptic Gospels—Matthew, Mark, and Luke—present a vivid and compelling portrait of the mission and ministry of Jesus. The mystery of Jesus as both human and divine is the starting point for the authors of these Gospels—often called the Evangelists—as they tell the story of God's Reign that has come among us as the Son of God Most High. The story proceeds from Jesus's baptism by John, through his miracles and teaching, to the story's dramatic culmination in Jesus's death and Resurrection. Jesus Christ's proclamation of the Reign of God is history's defining moment and calls humanity to enter into grace and salvation.

THE SCRIPTURES

> He put before them another parable: "The kingdom of heaven is like a mustard seed that someone took and sowed in his field; it is the smallest of all the seeds, but when it has grown it is the greatest of shrubs and becomes a tree, so that the birds of the air come and make nests in its branches." (Matthew 13:31–32)

PARABLES

> The Gospels frequently describe Jesus as teaching in parables. A parable is a literary form that uses a fictional story to make a point. Many of Jesus's parables are like riddles. They have surprising or shocking endings designed to tease the people of his time into examining certain beliefs they took for granted. Unfortunately, the surprise of Jesus's parables is hard for some of us to understand today because we may be unfamiliar with the examples he used: baking bread, planting crops, herding sheep, or fishing for our supper. Jesus also used parables to teach about God's Reign. These were often in the form of analogies comparing God's Reign to common things or events: "The kingdom of heaven is like . . ." Using parables, Jesus challenged powerful and educated people but was also understood by common people. (*THE CATHOLIC YOUTH BIBLE*, near Matthew 13:10)

Questions from Jesus

Write a question you think Jesus might ask you.

Passages from the Gospel of Mark

1:35–39	3:1–6	5:14–20	6:1–6
6:53–56	8:11–13	8:31–33	11:15–19
14:32–36	14:48–50	14:66–72	15:33–37

Prayer of a Servant Leader

Dear Jesus, you made it clear that those who are greatest are the ones who serve, not the ones who have fame, fortune, or authority. Help me adjust my priorities to put others first. Place within me a genuine desire to serve. Enable me to recognize the daily opportunities I have to reach out to those in need in my family, in my school, and in my community. Guide me as I strive to follow your example to become a servant leader. Amen. (*The Catholic Youth Bible*, near Luke 22:24–27)

For Reflection

- Answer Jesus's question, "Who do you say I am?" from Matthew 16:15.

- Describe the Reign of God in common, everyday language.

- Why is it important to maintain balance in believing in Jesus as both fully God and fully human? What do we lose if we think of Jesus as only God? What do we lose if we think of him as only human?

- What are some practical ways you can make the Reign of God a priority?

- Which synoptic Gospel is your favorite? Why?

Live It!

- View the film *Godspell* (1973, 103 minutes, rated G) or *Jesus Christ Superstar* (1973, 108 minutes, rated G).
- Organize a collection of books, toiletries, and snacks for the local detention center.
- Keep a "Wise Sayings" journal and in it write important sayings from the Scriptures as well as from other sources.
- Invite your families to choose one "Kingdom activity" each month or even for the year. For example, have a soup supper once a month and then donate money to a shelter, pray the rosary as a family once a week, or attend Mass on Saturday morning once a month.

4
THE GOSPEL OF JOHN

The Gospel of John presents Jesus as the divine Son, the pre-existent Word. From the beginning of Jesus's ministry to the moment of his Crucifixion, he is powerful and in control, sent by God to triumphantly restore the world to right relationship with the Divine. The reader is called to live in the light of Jesus and so to share his eternal glory. But the call to be a disciple is an uncompromising one. Nothing short of total surrender is enough. "Love one another as I have loved you" sets the new standard for following Jesus Christ.

THE SCRIPTURES

> There was a man sent from God, whose name was John. He came as a witness, to testify to the light, so that all might believe through him. He himself was not the light, but he came to testify to the light. The true light, which enlightens everyone, was coming into the world. He was in the world, and the world came to be through him, yet the world did not know him. He came to what was his own, and his own people did not accept him. But to all who received him, who believed in his name, he gave power to become children of God, who were born not of blood or of the will of the flesh or of the will of man, but of God. And the Word became flesh and lived among us, and we have seen his glory, the glory as of a father's only Son, full of grace and truth. (John 1:6–14)

AT A GLANCE

Bible scholars usually divide the Book of John into the following four distinct sections:
- Prologue (1:1–18)
- Book of Signs (1:19–12:50)
- Book of Glory (chapters 13–20)
- Epilogue (chapter 21)

The Seven Signs
- Jesus attends the wedding at Cana (2:1–12).
- Jesus heals the official's son (4:46–54).
- Jesus heals on the Sabbath (5:1–18).
- Jesus feeds the five thousand (6:1–15).
- Jesus walks on water (6:16–21).
- The man born blind receives sight (9:1–41).
- Jesus raises Lazarus from the dead (11:1–44).

"I Am" Sayings of Jesus
"I am the bread of life" (John 6:35).
"I am the light of the world" (John 8:12).
"I am the gate for the sheep" (John 10:7).
"I am the good shepherd" (John 10:11).
"I am the resurrection and the life" (John 11:25).
"I am the way, and the truth, and the life" (John 14:6).
"I am the vine, you are the branches" (John 15:5).
- In what context did Jesus make each statement? That is, what was going on in the paragraphs before he made each "I am" statement?

The Eucharist
Jesus calls himself the "bread of life" (John 6:35). Some type of bread is part of the basic diet of almost every culture. Thus, in a symbolic way, Jesus is telling us that he is part of the basic diet for spiritual life. And just as bread is shared and valued in every culture, Jesus shares himself with all people who are willing to believe. Many of Jesus's early followers were troubled when he taught that they must eat his flesh and drink his blood in order to have true life (verses 56–60). The confusion and arguing among his listeners is understandable; his words must have sounded strange. Yet this teaching about the body and blood of Christ (which is portrayed in the Last Supper in Matthew, Mark, and Luke) is central to the Catholic faith. Catholics believe that Jesus is really present with us and nourishes us when we celebrate the Eucharist together, the bread and wine being changed into the body and blood of Christ. In your prayer, reflect or journal on the following questions: How is Jesus a source of nourishment for you? How does celebrating the Eucharist help you recognize more clearly Jesus's presence? How are you called to be the body and blood of Christ to the world around you? (*The Catholic Youth Bible*, near John, chapter 6)

- Is this passage or a statement like it found in any other Gospel?

- What reaction did Jesus receive from his disciples? the Jewish leaders? the general audience?

FOR REFLECTION

- Spend some time journaling to Jesus, the Bread of Life. Some possible questions you might answer in your journal are these: How can I be bread for others? How do I need to be nourished in my life of faith? For what do I really hunger?

- In the Gospel of John, Jesus's miracles are signs that point to the meaning of his life and his message. What signs of God's love and your call to be a disciple of Jesus are in your life?

- Jesus says, "I am the way, and the truth, and the life" (John 14:6). Share some ways Jesus has guided your way, provided you with truth, and been a source of life for you.

Live It!

- Search the Internet for images of Jesus. Decide whether each image emphasizes Jesus's humanity or his divinity.
- Spend time with your family or a group of friends making peanut butter and jelly sandwiches for people who are homeless. Require that each person bring a jar of either peanut butter or jelly. Organize a trip to deliver the sandwiches to a soup kitchen or shelter.
- Establish a family ritual for welcoming people to your home.
- Discuss with your family some events that serve as signs of God's love and care. Is there someone close to the family who serves as a special sign of the presence of Christ or God's love?

5

ACTS AND GALATIANS:
THE UNIVERSALITY OF CHRISTIANITY

In the first years after Pentecost, the young Church experienced amazing growth. The Apostles were on fire with the Holy Spirit, preaching and baptizing, with Jews and Gentiles alike seeking to follow Jesus Christ. But don't think for a moment that everything was perfect. From the outset the Church faced difficulties and even internal conflict. Yet the growth continued, and the Church was guided by the Spirit to work through those difficult times. The Gospel message was clear: All are welcome. Christianity invites every person to know and follow Jesus Christ.

THE SCRIPTURES

He saw heaven opened and something like a large sheet coming down, being lowered to the ground by its four corners. In it were all kinds of four-footed creatures and reptiles and birds of the air. Then he heard a voice saying, "Get up, Peter, kill and eat." But Peter said, "By no means, Lord; for I have never I eaten anything that is profane and unclean." The voice said to him again, a second time, "What God has made clean, you must not call profane." This happened three times, and the thing was suddenly taken up to heaven. Now while Peter was greatly puzzled about what to make of the vision that he had seen, suddenly the men sent by Cornelius appeared. They were asking for Simon's house and were standing by the gate. They called out to ask whether Simon, who was called Peter, was staying there. (Acts 10:11–18)

UNITY IN FAITH AND LOVE

When Paul and Barnabas were in Antioch, a controversy arose regarding the need for Gentiles to be circumcised and to follow certain Jewish laws and holidays. The earliest Christians were Jews. They believed in Jesus and continued to follow the rules of the Jewish faith as a sign that they were a Covenant people. But with Gentiles becoming Christians, new questions were raised, like: Do Gentiles have to follow all the Jewish rules? Do Gentiles need to be circumcised as a sign of the Covenant? Circumcision is the surgical removal of the foreskin from a penis, and the Gentile converts did not see the need for it. Paul and Barnabas insisted that Christians were free from such Jewish laws; they went to Jerusalem to meet with the other Apostles to defend their position. With Peter's support, Paul and Barnabas's view won the day. This meeting of the Apostles is called the Council of Jerusalem and was a pivotal point in the history of the Church. At it, the Apostles decided that the center of the Christian faith was believing in the risen Christ, not conforming to a Jewish ritual. How does your youth group or parish handle conflict? Does it handle it better when members remind themselves that they are united by their faith in Jesus? (*The Catholic Youth Bible*, near Acts 15:1–35)

Here Comes Everybody

The word *catholic* means "universal." Someone once described being Catholic as, "Here comes everybody!" In Acts 10:34–36, we hear that because God shows no partiality, neither should we. Even so, it is sometimes easier to stick with people who are similar to us. They understand us and know where we are coming from. There's less explaining to do. Right? But being Catholic means reaching out of our familiar circle of friends and including in our group people of different cultures and religions. Have you ever seen a Native American blanket? Threads of various colors are woven together to form an intricate, new pattern. Each blanket is completely different from every other blanket. By building relationships with people of different cultures and embracing their diversity, we become like one of the threads in such a blanket, weaving our uniquenesses in a new and beautiful pattern. The result is different and enriching, and then we become truly Catholic. (*The Catholic Youth Bible*, near Acts 10:34–36)

The Journeys of Paul

According to most interpretations of Acts, Paul made three missionary journeys over a ten-year period to spread the Gospel message. The details of his first journey are covered in chapters 13–14. The second journey is reported in chapters 16–18. The third journey is described in chapters 19–21. Paul himself may have seen these not as three separate journeys but as one continuous missionary activity. On these journeys, Paul made converts and started Christian communities. On the second and third journeys, he also visited established communities to give them guidance and support. Paul's third journey landed him back in Jerusalem, where some Jews had him arrested. On the basis of his Roman citizenship, Paul appealed to the emperor. So he was transported to Rome (this trip is referred to as his fourth journey). He probably died there as a martyr around AD 65. Some traditions say that Paul wasn't martyred there but went on to evangelize in Spain. (*The Catholic Youth Bible*, near Acts of the Apostles, chapters 13–21)

Help Us Evangelize

O God, how I admire Paul! I too want to share your Good News with my generation. So let your Holy Spirit bless me with the gift of evangelization. Help me reach out to other young people no matter what clique or group they belong to. Help me to bring out the best in our culture and to challenge that which is wrong or misleading. Give me courage to speak fearlessly about my faith in Jesus when it is right to do so. And let me be your instrument in building communities of faith, hope, and love. Amen. (Adapted from THE CATHOLIC YOUTH BIBLE, near Acts of the Apostles, chapter 17.)

Fill Me, Lord!

Fill me with the fruits of your Spirit, Lord.
Fill me with love, so that I seek to
    understand and appreciate the rich
    variety and diversity of life that
    surrounds me.
Fill me with joy, so that I celebrate your
    presence in each and every moment I am
    on this earth.
Fill me with peace, so that I know how to
    ease those angry and sometimes violent
    urges that well up inside of me.
Fill me with patience, so that I stop rushing
    long enough to witness your miraculous
    work taking place all around me (and
    within me!).
Fill me with kindness, so that I take the
    extra time to help the one in need, even
    when it isn't convenient for me.
Fill me with faithfulness, so that I place
    my mind, heart, and all that I do in the
    service of your Gospel.
Fill me with gentleness, so that others know
    that I believe in a God who loves and
    cares for all people.

Fill me with self-control, so that I act not
    on my impulses and urges, but rather on
    my beliefs and values, which are rooted in
    you.
Fill me with these fruits of your spirit, Lord!
    Amen.

(This prayer is from THE CATHOLIC YOUTH BIBLE, near Galatians 5:22–26.)

FOR REFLECTION

- Write a journal entry asking the Holy Spirit for the grace to be more open and welcoming to all you meet, especially other young people who are ignored or not accepted at school.

- Ask for guidance from Christ about the vocation God is calling you to. Do this by journaling about the priesthood, religious life, and marriage. Are you open to all these vocations? Do you feel more strongly called to one of these vocations?

Live It!

- Set up a road trip to visit various local parishes that were founded to serve a particular ethnic community in the past (Irish, Polish, German, and so on) or that serve African Americans or recent immigrants (Mexican and Vietnamese, for example). Ideally, find several parishes in the same neighborhood.

- Check out different Web sites of dioceses around the country, as well as the Vatican Web site and those of other dioceses around the world.

- Rent and view the film *The Mission* (1986, 126 minutes, rated PG).

- Discuss with your family the ideas of freedom and responsibility. How do your parents view freedom? Do they have less freedom now that they are married with children? What concerns do they have about your increasing freedom and independence?

- Have a family mission collection during Advent or Lent. Create a mission bowl or can. At a weekly designated meal, have each person in your family make a contribution using leftover lunch money, allowance, and so on. Say a special prayer for all missionaries around the world at the end of the meal. Send all the money collected to the missions of your choice.

6

ROMANS AND JAMES: FAITH

Catholics define faith as both God's grace and our vocation. As God's grace it is the most fundamental gift God gives us. We cannot think or will ourselves to have faith. It is God's initiative, God who first gives himself so that we can believe. But we must take care, because like any gift faith can become a mere showpiece, something appreciated for a while and then set aside.

This is why Christian faith is also a vocation, a call to a way of life. The gift of faith demands that we place our trust and our surrender in the power of God in Jesus Christ. Authentic faith shapes the heart of the believer and takes us deeper into the heart of God.

THE SCRIPTURES

> But now, apart from the law, the righteousness of God has been disclosed and is attested by the law and the prophets, the righteousness of God through faith in Jesus Christ for all who believe. For there is no distinction, since all have sinned and fall short of the glory of God; they are now justified by his grace as a gift, through the redemption that is in Christ Jesus, whom God put forward as a sacrifice of atonement by his blood, effective through faith. He did this to show his righteousness, because in his divine forbearance he had passed over the sins previously committed; it was to prove at the present time that he himself is righteous and that he justifies the one who has faith in Jesus. Then what becomes of boasting? It is excluded. By what law? By that of works? No, but by the law of faith. For we hold that a person is justified by faith apart from works prescribed by the law. Or is God the God of Jews only? Is he not the God of Gentiles also? Yes, of Gentiles also, since God is one; and he will justify the circumcised on the ground of faith and the uncircumcised through that same faith. Do we then overthrow the law by his faith? By no means! On the contrary, we uphold the law. (Romans 3:21–31)

THE LAW, FAITH, AND SALVATION

Throughout much of Romans, Paul is explaining the relationship between the Law, faith, and salvation. At the end of chapter 2 and the beginning of chapter 3, he shows that the Jewish Law of the Old Testament cannot save us from the effect of sin. But he recognizes the value of the Law (see 3, 31). The Law was the expression of the Jewish people's response of faith to God's Covenant. It protected their relationships with God and one another. We often think of sin as breaking God's law. But at its core, sin is really breaking our relationship with God and distancing ourselves from God. Remember what Adam and Eve did after their first sin? They hid from God, ashamed of their action. Paul is clear that we are all guilty of sin. Separated from God, the source of all life, we would eventually perish without God's help. But God is always seeking us out. In the ultimate act of love, God sent Jesus to restore the break in our relationship caused by sin. Jesus's death and Resurrection show us that God's great love is far more powerful than any sin we can commit. Paul uses two key words to explain all of this. He talks about *justification*, which is the process that brings us back into a good relationship with God. And he talks about *righteousness* as the state of being right with God, of not being separated from God. How are we justified? How are we considered righteous? Not by our ability to keep any laws but by our faith in Jesus Christ. And the effect of faith is opposite that of sin. Where sin creates distance, faith draws us close. Where sin kills, faith gives life. Where sin shrivels in hate, faith is active in love. (THE CATHOLIC YOUTH BIBLE, near Romans 3:21–31)

FAITH VERSUS GOOD WORKS

Ephesians 2:1–10 deals with the question of faith versus good works (good works are moral living and Gospel-motivated works of service, justice, courage, and so on). This issue has divided Christians since the early Church and was a major issue at the time of the Protestant Reformation. Some say that we are saved by our good works. Others say good works are irrelevant, and we are saved only through our faith in Christ. The writer of Ephesians makes it clear that both those statements are incomplete. The core Christian belief is this: We are saved by God's grace through faith in Jesus Christ. We are saved not by doing good works but in order to do good works. Our salvation is God's gift to us; how we live is our gift to God. (THE CATHOLIC YOUTH BIBLE, near Ephesians 2:1–10)

The Tongue: Friend or Foe?

Sometimes, we are advised to hold it. Other times, we are ordered to bite it. Try as we may to keep this counsel, our tongue often proves to be much stronger than our will to control it. All of us have said things that we later regretted. Frequently against our better judgment, we find ourselves speaking in ways that hurt or offend others and God. People are injured by what others say to—or about—them, far more often than by physical attack. The scars left by hurtful words can last a lifetime, destroying families and ruining friendships. How have you used your tongue lately? Have you spoken words that are hurtful to another person, directly or behind the person's back? How might you use your tongue to begin to heal someone's hurts? Apologies, compliments, and affirmations—the tongue can utter these things too! It is a mark of maturity and confidence when we are able to ask forgiveness or affirm others. Christians are called to this kind of courage and maturity. Use your tongue to speak positively to others today! (*The Catholic Youth Bible*, near James 3:1–12)

God, When I Am Searching

God,
When I am searching for a reason to believe, lead me on the way of belief. Help me not to doubt you or your ways. When I am reluctant to practice my faith, give me encouragement in this time of doubtfulness. When I am angry and confused about why I tend to believe rather than not believe, help me to feel comfortable making my beliefs my own and to respect others' beliefs also.
Amen.

(Sara Koves, *More Dreams Alive*, page 97)

For Reflection

- How can we effectively give witness to our faith? Give examples of how people can witness without being obnoxious.

- Write a journal entry asking the Holy Spirit to keep watch over your words. Seek forgiveness for the times you have spoken evil about someone, and ask for strength to speak in the face of sin and injustice.

- Keep a list of times or situations when you offer some kind of visible witness to your faith and of those times when you let the opportunity to give witness slip by. Be sure to check your progress at the end of each week.

Live It!

- Create prayers of blessing for your parents, siblings, friends, schoolmates, and others, and offer them as gifts or affirmations to the people you love.
- Invite some friends or family members to watch the classic version of the film *Miracle on 34th Street* (1947, 96 minutes, rated G). Discuss the nature of faith and the obstacles to the faith experienced by young people.
- Interview your parents about why they are thankful for the gift of faith.

7

THE BOOK OF REVELATION: OUR ULTIMATE DESTINY

The first followers of Jesus did not have an easy time. At best they were ignored and misunderstood. Often, however, during the first two centuries of the Church's existence, they faced violence, persecution, and death. The Book of Revelation, written in the genre of apocalyptic literature, uses symbols, fantastic images, and the promise of God's ultimate victory to bolster the faith of the Church. As those early Christians struggled to remain faithful, they were both comforted and challenged by the example of Jesus Christ. His victory is our victory. His destiny is ours: life forever in the kingdom of justice, power, truth, love, and glory.

THE SCRIPTURES

> The revelation of Jesus Christ, which God gave to him to show his servants what must soon take place, he made it known by sending his angel to his servant John, who testified to the word of God and to the testimony of Jesus Christ, even to all that he saw. Blessed is the one who reads aloud the words of the prophecy, and blessed are those who hear and keep what is written in it; for the time is near. (Revelation 1:1–13)

MAJOR PERSECUTIONS IN THE EARLY CHURCH

- **Nero's Persecution, AD 64 (Rome).** The emperor Nero used the prejudice against Christians to blame them for a catastrophic fire in the city. It is commonly held that both Peter and Paul died during this persecution.
- **Domitian's Persecution, AD 81–96 (Rome).** The emperor Domitian demanded to be honored and worshiped as a god. His was a terrible persecution that spread to other parts of the empire and lasted for many years.
- **Trajan's Persecution, AD 98–117.** Throughout the empire, being a Christian was considered a crime punishable by death. Christians were not hunted, but if they were discovered, they had to renounce their faith or be executed.
- **Decius's Persecution, AD 249–251.** All citizens were required to carry a certificate saying that they had paid homage to the gods. Christians who could not prove they had done so faced death. Apostasy, denying one's faith, was frequent, as many Christians had to deny their faith in order to save their lives.

- **Diocletian's Persecution, AD 284–305.** During this final and most brutal of the persecutions, many Christians lost their lives as well as their property. The emperor tried to remove all Christianity from the empire.

(This material is adapted from Michael Pennock, *The Catholic Church Story,* pages 51–54.)

Apocalyptic Literature

Apocalypse is a Greek word meaning "to uncover or reveal." Apocalyptic literature is written to sound like an attempt to foretell the future by using symbols and visions. But the symbols are often codes for people and events in the present. This type of literature frequently is produced during a time of persecution, when using real names could get a person into trouble or even killed. Apocalyptic literature developed in Israel around 200 BC when the country was enduring great persecution and suffering. The Book of Revelation in the New Testament is another example of apocalyptic literature. The Book of Daniel contains some explanation of the visions it describes. But sometimes, you will have to consult a good Bible commentary (a book that gives additional background on Bible passages) to completely understand the symbols. For instance, you might need help recognizing that the four beats in chapter 7 are symbols for Babylon, Media, Persia, and Greece—the four nations that ruled over Israel but would pass away. Or that the arrogant eleventh horn on the fourth beast's head is a symbol for Antiochus IV Epiphanes, the king who persecuted the Jews during the time Daniel was written. Apocalyptic literature assured the people of Israel that God would triumph and the present evil would eventually pass away. It was one more way to reinforce the belief that evil would be punished and good rewarded, even when it didn't look that way at the moment. (*The Catholic Youth Bible,* near Daniel, chapters 7–10)

Symbolism and Revelation

- What is the literal meaning? In one or two sentences, describe what your passage says without interpreting the symbols.

- Identify the main symbols of the passage.

- What is the meaning of the symbols? If necessary, consult a biblical commentary.

- Add other comments, if you have any.

The Memorare of St. Bernard of Clairvaux

Remember, most loving Virgin Mary,
never was it heard
that anyone who turned to you for help
was left unaided.

Inspired by this confidence,
though burdened by my sins,
I run to your protection,
for you are my mother.

Mother of the Word of God,
do not despise my words of pleading
but be merciful and hear my prayer.
Amen.

For Reflection

- How do you stay faithful when your commitment to Jesus Christ and his Church brings suffering, rejection, or ridicule?

- What are some difficulties young people and adults face in being part of the Catholic Church or of any Christian Church?

- Some early Christians were persecuted because they refused to participate in activities they felt would contribute to worshiping the emperor or false Gods. What activities, careers, or entertainment should Christians avoid?

- Some people believe that contemporary media is biased against people who have strong religious convictions. Do you agree? How are religious people and religious issues portrayed on television and in the movies you watch?

Live It!

- Search the Internet or visit a museum to discover what areas of the United States were settled because of religious persecution. For example, explore the histories of Maryland, Massachusetts, or Pennsylvania.
- Search the Internet for faith communities that face persecution and discrimination today. Check out the Web sites for the Catholic News Service, the Vatican, and other news service organizations.

- Write personal letters of support and concern to missionaries or youth groups of faith communities that face persecution and difficulty. For names and addresses of people you can write, contact Catholic Relief Services, the local Catholic Charities office, or a missionary community such as Maryknoll.
- Explore the history of anti-Semitism among Christian communities, especially Russia, Germany, and even the United States.

8

TRUTH IN THE BIBLE

The question of truth in the Bible has been discussed for centuries. Most Christians agree that the Bible teaches God's truth, but they find it difficult to come to a common definition of God's truth. The historical critical method of interpreting the Bible influenced scholars in the late nineteenth century. The emphasis this approach places on literary genres, historical background, and the author's audience is controversial. The Roman Catholic Church has played an essential role in the conversation. Catholics reject an extreme fundamentalism that insists that everything in the Bible is literally true, but the Catholic Church does insist that the word of God is without error in proclaiming the religious truth God intended for human salvation.

THE SCRIPTURES

> Then Pilate entered the headquarters again, summoned Jesus, and asked him, "Are you the King of the Jews?" Jesus answered, "Do you ask this on your own, or did others tell you about me?" Pilate replied, "I am not a Jew, am I? Your own nation and the chief priests have handed you over to me. What have you done?" Jesus answered, "My kingdom is not from this world. If my kingdom were from this world, my followers would be fighting to keep me from being handed over to the Jews. But as it is, my kingdom is not from here." Pilate asked him, "So you are a king?" Jesus answered, "You say that I am a king. For this I was born, and for this I came into the world, to testify to the truth. Everyone who belongs to the truth listens to my voice." Pilate asked him, "What is truth?" After he had said this, he went out to the Jews again and told them, "I find no case against him. But you have a custom that I release someone for you at the Passover. Do you want me to release for you the King of the Jews?" They shouted in reply, "Not this man, but Barabbas!" Now Barabbas was a bandit. (John 18:33–38)

THE HOLY SPIRIT GUIDES US INTO ALL TRUTH!

> Jesus told his disciples that after his death, God would send the Spirit of Truth to be with them forever. Jesus calls the Holy Spirit the Advocate (see John 16:7), the one who defends us from evil and sin. The Holy Spirit also guides us into all Truth, by helping us to grasp the meaning of Jesus's words, actions, and miracles. (*THE CATHOLIC YOUTH BIBLE*, near John 14:15–31, 16:5–15)

TRUTH IN THE BIBLE

TYPES OF TRUTH

STATEMENTS	METHOD OF VERIFYING	TYPE OF TRUTH	OFFICIAL RATING	EXPLANATION FOR OFFICIAL RATING
Winona, Minnesota, is 100 miles south of Minneapolis.	Check a map or drive yourself.	Geographic	+	Archaeologists have found evidence supporting many of the statements in the Bible relating to geography. However, some statements are inaccurate because the writer had incomplete knowledge or wished to make a religious point.
The Declaration of Independence was signed in 1776.	Look in an encyclopedia or history book.	Historical	+	Many historical references in the Bible are accurate and correspond to archaeological evidence that has been discovered in modern times. However, biblical authors sometimes adjusted the sequence of events to make a religious truth stand out.
Water is composed of hydrogen and oxygen molecules.	Perform an observation, perhaps using special instruments.	Scientific	–	The biblical writers reflected the scientific knowledge of their time, which by our standards was primitive and inaccurate. Who knows what people living a thousand years from now will think of our scientific knowledge?
Cheating is wrong.	Examine the accumulated experience of society and your own personal experience of hurt or harm.	Moral	++	The Bible is filled with moral teaching. Jesus raised the standard of moral truth. This does not mean that the moral truth taught before Jesus's time was inaccurate, only that it was incomplete.
The trees swayed and the flowers danced to the music of the wind.	Use intuition and imagination.	Symbolic	++	Much of the truth in the Bible is taught symbolically, through parables, myths, and metaphors. We may have to work to understand and appreciate the meaning of a symbol, but once we do, we can comprehend the truth it reveals.
God's love is for all people.	Review the accumulated experience of society and your own personal experience of God.	Religious	++	The Bible is primarily about religious truth. What it reveals about the nature of God, Jesus, and the Holy Spirit—and our relationship with them—is always true and can always be counted on.

(This activity is adapted from Brian Singer-Towns, *The Bible: Power and Promise*, page 100.)

Nothing But the Truth

"Do you swear to tell the truth, the whole truth, and nothing but the truth, so help you God?" We have all heard these words. They are asked of every witness about to testify in a courtroom. In addition to responding positively to this crucial question, witnesses are called to place a hand on the Bible. All of this is to try to ensure that they will be honest. But despite this oath, some witnesses lie. We call that crime perjury, and it carries a severe penalty because someone's innocence or guilt may be hanging on the sworn testimony. Proverbs 10:18 tells us, "Lying lips conceal hatred." Just as dishonesty is an act of hatred, so is honesty an act of love. Ultimately, our lies end up hurting others and damaging our integrity. Whether in the courtroom, or in everyday life, we must always strive to tell "the truth, the whole truth, and nothing but the truth." (*The Catholic Youth Bible,* near Proverbs 10:18–21)

For Reflection

- How can I best be true to the person the Holy Spirit is calling me to be?

- Reflect on a time when being honest cost you something: money, pride, or maybe even a friendship. Why does being honest sometimes come with a cost?

- Why is it important to believe that the Bible is without error in teaching us the truth that God wants us to know for salvation?

- Do you find it hard to accept that the Bible might not be accurate in scientific and historic details but still without error in religious truth? Why or why not?

Live It!

- Generate a list of twenty-five people you believe are absolutely truthful.
- As a family, search the Internet for ways that propaganda has been used by governments throughout history. Discuss the responsibility that citizens have to call their elected officials to give honest accounts of their actions and decisions.

Acknowledgments

The scriptural quotations contained herein are from the New Revised Standard Version of the Bible, Catholic Edition. Copyright © 1993 and 1989 by the Division of Christian Education of the National Council of the Churches of Christ in the United States of America. All rights reserved.

Excerpted or adapted material labeled THE CATHOLIC YOUTH BIBLE is from THE CATHOLIC YOUTH BIBLE, revised edition (Winona, MN: Saint Mary's Press, 2005). Copyright © 2005 by Saint Mary's Press. All rights reserved.

The prayer by Sara Koves on page 33 is from More Dreams Alive: Prayers by Teenagers, edited by Carl Koch (Winona, MN. Saint Mary's Press, 1995), page 97. Copyright © 1995 by Saint Mary's Press. All rights reserved.

The bulleted items on pages 35–36 are adapted from The Catholic Church Story, by Michael Pennock (Notre Dame, IN: Ave Maria Press, 1991), pages 51–54. Copyright © 1991 by Ave Maria Press.

The "Memorare of St. Bernard of Clairvaux" on page 37 was verified against an authoritative source.

The activity on page 41 is adapted from The Bible: Power and Promise, by Brian Singer-Towns (Winona, MN: Saint Mary's Press, 1997), page 100. Copyright © 1997 by Saint Mary's Press. All rights reserved.

During this book's preparation, all citations, facts, figures, names, addresses, telephone numbers, Internet URLs, and other pieces of information cited within were verified for accuracy. The authors and Saint Mary's Press staff have made every attempt to reference current and valid sources, but we cannot guarantee the content of any source, and we are not responsible for any changes that may have occurred since our verification. If you find an error in, or have a question or concern about, any of the information or sources listed within, please contact Saint Mary's Press.

JOURNALING PAGE

JOURNALING PAGE

JOURNALING PAGE

Journaling Page